4,70

THE GROUND OF THE CHURCH AND THE MEETINGS OF THE CHURCH

WITNESS LEE

Living Stream Ministry
Anaheim, CA

© 2002 Living Stream Ministry

All rights reserved. No part of this work may be reproduced or transmitted in any form or by any means—graphic, electronic, or mechanical, including photocopying, recording, or information storage and retrieval systems—without written permission from the publisher.

First Edition, February 2002.

ISBN 0-7363-1562-4

Published by

Living Stream Ministry
2431 W. La Palma Ave., Anaheim, CA 92801 U.S.A.
P. O. Box 2121, Anaheim, CA 92814 U.S.A.

Printed in the United States of America

02 03 04 05 06 07 08 / 10 9 8 7 6 5 4 3 2 1

CONTENTS

Title	Page
Preface	5
1 The Ground of the Church	7
2 Practicing the Body Life on the Proper Ground of Oneness	19
3 The Christian Meetings as a Testimony of the Enjoyment of Christ in Our Daily Life	33
4 Four Main Items in the Lord's Table Meeting	45
5 Practical Points concerning the Lord's Table Meeting	51

PREFACE

This book is composed of messages given by Brother Witness Lee in Los Angeles, California in the summer training of 1965. These messages were not reviewed by the speaker. The subject of the summer training was the inner life and the church life. The messages in this book were given concurrently with messages on the growth in life and the function of life, including the messages published as *Christ as the Content of the Church and the Church as the Expression of Christ* and *The Enjoyment of Christ*.

CHAPTER ONE

THE GROUND OF THE CHURCH

Scripture Reading: Eph. 4:4-6; Acts 8:1; 13:1; Rev. 1:11; 2:1; 1 Cor. 1:2; Rom. 1:7

There are many important matters related to the church life, but the first two main items for our practice and experience are the content of the church and the standing, or the ground, of the church. The content of the church is Christ, not merely in teaching or doctrine, but in practice, reality, and experience. Christ as the very life, content, and everything for the church is the basic, main, and first aspect of the church life. What we are practicing is not something in vain according to a form or certain teaching. We are practicing a life with Christ as its very life, content, and everything. The church life, the life of the church, the practice of the church life, is a life with Christ as everything.

The second main point of the church life is the standing, the ground, of the church. In order to build a house, there are two items that are most important: the materials and the site. When someone builds a house, he first must decide what material he will use to build it. A house can be built with cement, stone, wood, adobe, or even gold. Second, he must decide in what place, on what ground, he will build, whether on a mountain, by a river, or in the plain. For the building of the church, Christ as life is the material, the content. On what ground, then, on what standing, should we have the church life? We are building the church as the house, even the temple, so where must we build it? Can we build the temple in Babylon, Egypt, Syria, or somewhere else?

According to the revelation of the Scriptures, the ground of the church is very important. This is particularly true in the

Old Testament types of the church. In the Old Testament no one dared to build the temple in any place he chose. There was only one place, the place chosen and appointed by God. For a thousand years, not one Israelite dared to build a temple in any place that he liked, because all the Jews realized that there was only one place, one site, where they could build the temple legally and properly. To build the temple in any other place, no matter what kind of temple it was, would be illegal. It would not be proper because it was not on the proper ground. We have to be very clear about this matter.

THE DIFFERENCE BETWEEN THE FOUNDATION OF THE CHURCH AND THE GROUND OF THE CHURCH

In at least the first eight or ten years of my Christian life, I did not know what the ground of the church was. I never saw such a term in the writings and messages in Christianity. The term *church ground* was first used by Brother Watchman Nee in 1937. Before that time, this matter was not very clear, and this term was not in use. I hope that we all can be clear about the word *ground*. We use this word with a meaning that is different from *foundation*. The foundation is the basic part of the construction of a building. The ground, however, is not a part of the construction. It is the place, the piece of land, the site, the standing, on which the foundation is laid. We can construct a building with its foundation on a certain site or lot, or we may construct the same building with the same foundation on another lot. The building with the address 1101, for example, could have been built at the address 1103. By the term *ground,* we refer to the lot, the site on which we build. A lot is the site, and upon this site we place a foundation; then upon the foundation we construct a building. This is what we mean by the ground of the church.

In the large city of Los Angeles, for example, there is a big entity called the Catholic Church. The Catholic Church claims to be built upon Christ as the foundation. There is another entity called the Presbyterian Church that makes the same claim, that it is built upon Christ as the foundation. Likewise, the Baptists, the Methodists, and the Episcopalians also claim the same thing, that Christ is their cornerstone and foundation. It is the same with the Church of Christ and the Nazarenes. Not one of the so-called Christian churches fails to claim that Christ is their foundation. All have Christ as their foundation, but they have neglected the proper ground of the church.

The Catholic Church claims to be built upon Christ as its foundation, but this building is on a particular ground, the ground of Roman Catholicism. The Presbyterian Church also claims to be a building upon Christ as the foundation, but this building is upon the ground of the presbytery. Likewise, the Southern Baptist Church claims to be built on Christ as the foundation, but it is built on the ground of baptism, just as the Lutheran Church is built on the ground of Luther. All are so-called churches with the same foundation, that is, Christ; however, all are built upon different grounds. It is the grounds that create trouble. If the Roman Catholics would be willing to give up the ground of Roman Catholicism, the Presbyterians to give up the ground of the presbytery, and the Southern Baptists to give up the ground of baptism, eventually and spontaneously they all would be one. Then there will be no division. If we remove all the different names and different grounds of the denominations, what is left will simply be the church in Los Angeles with Christ and all the saints, without divisions or denominations. There will be no separating lines between us. There will be saints of one kind with one Christ to form one unique church in Los Angeles, composed together to be built up upon Christ as the foundation and standing on the local ground as the local church in Los Angeles.

ALL THE MINISTRIES BUILDING UP THE CHURCH ON THE PROPER GROUND

We may use the city of Corinth as an example. Paul went to Corinth to preach the gospel and to do the work of the Lord, but Paul did not set up a Pauline church with Christ as the foundation. Apollos went there also, but neither did he set up a church with Christ as the foundation and Apollos as the ground. In the same way, Peter did not set up a church with

Christ as the foundation and Peter as the ground to establish a Petrine church. In Corinth there was neither a Pauline church, a Petrine church, or a church of Apollos. Paul went to Corinth, preached the gospel, brought many people to the Lord, and established a church with Christ as the foundation on the local ground of Corinth. Paul established a local church there, and when Apollos went to Corinth, he did not set up another church. He simply brought more people to the Lord and built them on the same ground. Peter brought another number of people to the Lord, but neither did he set up another church. Peter built up those people on the same ground.

Therefore, in Corinth there was only one church, built with Christ as the unique foundation and located in the city of Corinth as the unique ground. Thus, there was the church in Corinth. First Corinthians 1:1 and 2a say, "Paul, a called apostle of Christ Jesus through the will of God, and Sosthenes the brother, to the church of God which is in Corinth." Paul did not say, "To the churches of God which are in Corinth" but "To the church of God which is in Corinth," the one church, singular in number. Paul went to Corinth, Apollos went there, and Peter went there. These different ministers with their ministries went to Corinth, but they all built one church with Christ as the foundation on the one unique ground, the ground of oneness, the ground of locality.

Therefore, eventually there was only one church, the church in Corinth. There were not more than one church: a Pauline church, a Petrine church, and a church of Apollos. There was not even a so-called church of Christ, in the divisive sense (v. 12). There was only one church, built with saints of one kind on one foundation—Christ—and upon one unique ground, the ground of oneness in the locality where that church was. There was one church, one foundation, and one ground. This is very clear.

Someone may say, "Yes, in Los Angeles there are the Catholic Church, the Presbyterian Church, the Baptist Church, and others, all on different kinds of ground. Not only so, here we also have many free groups, without any ground." However, if someone meets without a ground, where can he stand?

Even a small man needs at least a square foot of earth to stand upon. Just as no one can float in the air, there cannot be a free group that has no ground. Some free groups do not have a written, declared, or designated ground, but they have some kind of ground that is understood. Every kind of free group has a ground. To say that they take no ground is to be cheated and deceived.

By this we can see the difference between the foundation and the ground. Today the problem is not with the foundation; the problem is with the ground. This is why we say that in order to practice the church life, we must consider the ground as the second main item of the church. By the grace of the Lord, we are endeavoring to give up any other kind of ground and take the unique ground of oneness, the ground of locality. This is the only ground of the church.

THE GOVERNING PRINCIPLE
OF THE ONENESS OF THE CHURCH

The ground of the church can be seen both in the Old Testament types and in the New Testament revelation. We have the church in Corinth, for example, and the seven churches in Revelation 2 and 3. The oneness of the church can also be seen in the testimony of the physical universe, and it can be seen in the New Jerusalem. All these types and examples point out that the church is built upon one unique ground.

The church is the Body of Christ. The governing principle and rule is that one head always has one body. One head cannot have more than one body. Since the church is the Body of Christ, and Christ is the one Head, so the church must be one, and the church is one. That is why Ephesians 4:4 through 6 speaks of one Body, one Spirit, one hope, one Lord, one faith, one baptism, and one God and Father. With the church, everything is one because the church is one.

THE TESTIMONY OF ONENESS
IN THE PHYSICAL UNIVERSE

In the whole universe there is only one church. We may compare the church to the moon. In the whole universe the earth has only one moon. Someone may ask, then, why the

New Testament speaks of so many churches. It is because these many churches are the churches in many cities, many localities. In the universe the church is one, but the expression of the church is on this earth and among the human communities. In one city there is an expression of the church, which is called the local church, the church in a certain city. Then in another city there is another expression of the church, which is called the church in that city. The church in the universe is one, but the expressions of the church on this earth are many, in many cities. However, we still have the principle that the expression of the church in each city must be unique.

THE EXAMPLES OF THE GROUND OF THE CHURCH IN THE NEW TESTAMENT

This is why in the city of Jerusalem there was one church, the church in Jerusalem. Acts 8:1 says, "And there occurred in that day a great persecution against the church which was in Jerusalem." There was only one church, the unique church in Jerusalem. Originally there were one hundred twenty believers in Jerusalem. Then one day three thousand were added, and on another day five thousand were added. We have to believe that many more thousands were eventually added in. There may have been twenty or thirty thousand believers in that one city (5:14; 21:20). According to 2:46 and 5:42, those thousands did not meet in only one place; they met from house to house. There were many meetings, but not one meeting by itself became a church. Rather, all the meetings were one church.

After this, the testimony and gospel of the Lord spread from Jerusalem to Samaria and from Samaria to Antioch. As a result, how many churches were there in Antioch? Acts 13:1 begins, "Now there were in Antioch, in the local church, prophets and teachers." This verse speaks of the one church in Antioch. In Antioch there were a number of gifted persons, prophets and teachers such as Paul, Barnabas, and others. However, these gifted persons did not form many churches. They were all members of the same, one, unique church in Antioch. Therefore, in Antioch there was one church.

From Palestine the Lord's move went on to Asia Minor,

including Ephesus. How many churches were there in Ephesus? According to Revelation 1:11 and 2:1, all the believers in Ephesus were one church. This was true not only in Ephesus but in all the seven cities in Asia Minor. In each one of those cities there was only one church: one in Ephesus, one in Smyrna, one in Pergamos, one in Thyatira, one in Sardis, one in Philadelphia, and one in Laodicea. There is not one exception to this rule.

From there the Lord's move went to Europe, including Corinth. How many churches were there in Corinth? According to 1 Corinthians 1:2, there was only one. Likewise, in Rome there was only one church (Rom. 1:7). By this we can see that in the universe the church is one, and the expression of the church in each locality is also one.

We can compare this to the uniqueness of the United States. In the whole world there is only one United States, and anywhere there is an expression of the United States, that expression must be unique. This is why in London there is only one American embassy. Likewise, if you go to Tokyo or Hong Kong, you will find only one American embassy or consulate. There is no need for an American citizen to ask which consulate in Hong Kong to go to. If someone asks in this way, people will say that he is foolish. There is only one United States on this earth, so in Hong Kong there is only one American consulate. A person only needs to ask where the consulate in Hong Kong is. If there were two American consulates in Hong Kong, that would mean that the United States has been divided into two, and if there were three consulates in Hong Kong, the United States would have been divided into three.

When a person in Jerusalem was saved, he did not need to ask what church he should join, because there was only one church in Jerusalem. Before he was saved, he was outside the church. Now after being saved, he became a member of the one church there. At night if I tell a brother to look at the moon, he will not ask which moon to look at, because there is only one moon. In the same way, there is no need to consider to which church we should go—to the Presbyterian, Baptist, Nazarene, Lutheran, Methodist, or Episcopalian Church—because there is only one church.

For practical reasons, a brother may transfer from Jerusalem to Antioch. When he arrives, there is no need to ask to which church he should go. He must simply be in the church in Antioch. The only thing he needs to know is where the church has its meetings. Perhaps they are in one brother's home tonight and another brother's home the next night, but it is still one church. If the brother is later transferred to Ephesus, it is the same there. Again in Ephesus, the meeting of the church one night may be in one home and the next week in another home, but it is still one church. In Corinth, likewise, there is no need to consider whether the "Pauline" church is better than the "Petrine" church. There is no need to say, "I come from Jerusalem, so I know Peter better and will go to the Petrine church." There is no such Petrine church; there is only one church. Yet again, if the brother were to transfer from Corinth to Rome, it would be the same; there is only one church in Rome.

THE ULTIMATE WAY OF ONENESS IN THE NEW JERUSALEM

In the New Jerusalem there is one way, one street (Rev. 22:1). Because there is one street, no one can go astray. This one way saves us. There is no confusion and no possibility to go astray. Even if we try to go astray, we eventually will not be able to, because in the New Jerusalem there is only one way, and there will be no possibility to get off of it.

THE WAY OF DIVISIONS TODAY

How beautiful and how pleasant this picture is, just as Psalm 133:1 says, "Behold, how good and how pleasant it is / For brothers to dwell in unity!" Today in each city, however, the situation is different. Everywhere—in Los Angeles, San Francisco, Seattle, Tokyo, Taipei, and Hong Kong—people ask, "Are you a Christian? Have you been saved? Praise the Lord! What is your church?" An American brother may say, "I am of the Church of England," even though it seems foolish for an American citizen to be in an English church. If he is transferred to another city, he will look for the British church in that city. Similarly, a Chinese brother in America may say that he is in the Chinese Independent Church, and someone of Scandinavian descent may say he belongs to the Swedish Lutheran Church. In one American city there may be an Anglo church, a Chinese church, and a Swedish church. How strange this sounds, but this is exactly the situation. Here is a so-called church built upon the British ground, another built upon the Chinese ground, and another built upon the Swedish ground.

In the same way, a Japanese person may say he belongs to the Japanese Baptist Church. Someone who comes from Greece may not like the British, thinking they are too political. Neither does he like the Chinese, thinking they are too concerned with money, and he also does not like the Swedes and the Japanese. Because he likes only his countrymen, the Greeks, he will look for the Greek Orthodox Church, the church built upon the Greek ground. This is the situation today. We need a "vaccination" against this disease.

MEETING OUTSIDE THE MANY GROUNDS OF DIVISION

If someone asks what church we belong to, we should simply say, "I belong to the church." If he asks what kind of church that is, we can say, "It is simply the church." There are many small "circles" meeting in each city—the British circle, the Chinese circle, the Swedish circle, and the Japanese circle, as well as the Presbyterian, Baptist, Methodist, Episcopalian, and Lutheran circles. Where then should we place ourselves? We should be outside the circles, outside the camp (Heb. 13:13), and in the one "circle" of the church. The problem between brothers is due to the small circles. If we remove the small circles, we all will be in the one church. There will be no divisions, all of which come from the small circles. All these small circles become many different grounds upon which many different kinds of churches are built up.

If all the grounds were torn down, this would leave only one ground without any division. However, someone may say that there is no possibility of tearing down all these grounds. I agree with this; there is no possibility. According to the prophecy in the New Testament, the denominational grounds will remain until the Lord's coming. Not only is there no possibility of actually tearing them down; even the Lord Himself has no intention to get rid of them. The Lord will tolerate all these things, let them remain until He comes back, and then put them all under His judgment.

In such a situation full of confusion, however, where shall we stand? Can we stand in the various denominations? No we cannot. Can we stand in the national churches? No we cannot. We should stand simply on the ground of the locality where we are. I am a saint living in Los Angeles, so I should stand on the ground of this city, and so should many others. Then we can come together, but we do not "draw a small circle." We do not build upon another ground. Moreover, we do not specialize in anything but are very general. When these brothers and sisters who are outside the small circles come together, they are simply standing on the proper ground, the local ground, the ground of oneness.

LEARNING THE LESSONS OF THE CROSS AND OF THE LIMITATION OF GOD'S ORDINATION

If some new brothers come to a city, they may look at those brothers meeting on the proper ground and notice that they do not speak in tongues. Because of this, the new brothers may decide to have a separate meeting in their home where they can speak in tongues. Their meeting in the home becomes a tongues-speaking meeting. Then gradually they may bring more into this meeting, still claiming that they are not a denomination. In fact, however, they are a small sect. We have no right to do this. If we do, we will create a division, another small "circle," not being limited by the Lord's ordination and decision.

A number of brothers may be meeting together outside all the "circles," but gradually three or four may feel unhappy with the others and the meetings. They may feel that they can do something better, so they start to meet separately. In this way, these three or four create another small division. What then shall we do if we do not feel happy with the other brothers? The only thing to do is to learn the lessons of the cross and of limitation. We all have to be limited.

There is already an American embassy in Tokyo. Suppose

that when two men go to the embassy, the people there are not polite. Can those men start another embassy? Can they go back to their apartment and put a sign over it that says, "American Embassy"? If they do, they will be in trouble with the American government. They have no right to do that. How pitiful it is today, however. Wherever Christians go, they feel that they have the right, the liberty, the freedom, to do whatever they can. Today it is too easy to disagree with others and start a church in one's own home. It is easier than opening a new store. We cannot do this, and we have no right to do this. This is revealed by the type of the meeting in oneness in Deuteronomy 12. There was only one unique place appointed by God at which to worship the Lord (vv. 5-6, 11, 13-14). It was by that unique, appointed place that the oneness of the people of Israel was kept. One ground, one center, and one place kept the oneness.

Some may say that this concept is very good but too difficult to practice if there are thousands of believers in many meetings in one city. In actuality, this is not difficult. In a large city such as Los Angeles, there is one bank called The Bank of America. This one bank, however, may have up to one hundred branch offices. In the same way, there can be many meetings in one city, yet all the meetings are of one church, which is still the church in Los Angeles. Recently some brothers among us went to Taipei and saw the situation there. On the Lord's Day in Taipei there are up to forty meetings for the Lord's table, all meeting at the same time in the same city. All these home meetings, however, are of the one church in Taipei. If someone goes to Taipei, he may attend home meeting number one or home meeting number forty, but he is still attending the same church. There is no division there; rather, there is the oneness.

By this oneness there is the impact. If the fifty states of the United States were divided, the impact, the strength, and the power of this country would be lost. Why is the United States so strong today? It is because of the oneness. With the oneness there is the impact. Oh, how subtle the enemy is to divide the children of the Lord again and again! How weak the situation is today. There is no impact, and there is no learning of the lessons. If we keep the oneness, we will learn the lesson to recognize that each believer is our brother, and if we learn the lessons of the cross and of limitation, we will have the impact.

The ground of the church is not a small matter. It saves, keeps, and safeguards us, and it closes the back door for divisions. Regardless of whether or not we feel happy with someone, we have to meet with him on the proper ground. There is no other way and no other choice. There is only one choice, which is God's choice.

Chapter Two

PRACTICING THE BODY LIFE ON THE PROPER GROUND OF ONENESS

Scripture Reading: Deut. 12:5, 11, 13-14, 18a; 14:23; 15:20; 16:2, 6, 15-16

Some may ask why we pay so much attention to the ground of the church. It seems that it is not something related to the gospel, the inner life, the growth of life, or the Lord's glory. When we deal with anything, however, we need to have the insight to look into it, not only outwardly but even at its root. To see anything only outwardly is too childish and superficial. We do not want to be like children. If a wooden object has paint on the outside, it is not right to call that object "paint." The real item is wood, not paint; the paint is only on the surface. This illustrates that we must have the proper insight.

The enemy Satan is very subtle. Throughout all the past years he has been frustrating, blinding, and distracting God's people and even making many counterfeits. In these days, however, we are clear that God's intention, eternal purpose, and heart's desire are to work Christ into a group of people, to mingle Christ with them, and to build them up to be the living Body of Christ, His living expression, in all the communities where human beings live. God began this work after the resurrection and ascension of Christ, and He will realize it on this earth in this age. Of course, the ultimate consummation of the divine plan is the New Jerusalem. Before that time, however, God's intention is to have a living expression of His Son in this age, here and there in all the cities on this earth. This should not be hard for people to grasp; if we are not preoccupied, this vision from the Scriptures will be very clear. Regrettably, though, many Christians are not willing to be clear about this because they are preoccupied and distracted by something else.

THREE CATEGORIES OF SATAN'S FRUSTRATIONS TO THE CHURCH

Substitutes for Christ

The church has almost two thousand years of history. In these two thousand years we can see many things that the enemy has done. From the beginning of the church life, the enemy came in to frustrate, damage, distract, and make counterfeits of God's plan. All the things the enemy has done fall into three categories. The first category is the substitutes for Christ. Consider how many substitutes for Christ there are. Christ is the center, the reality, and all in all to God's chosen and elect people. The book of Colossians, however, was written because at that time human philosophy had become a substitute for Christ. Of all the human inventions, the best item was philosophy, including Gnosticism. God's intention is to work Christ into His chosen people, but the enemy utilized the best invention of human civilization to substitute for Christ. Therefore, the apostle Paul told the Colossians that Christ is the allotted portion of the saints and that Christ must be all in all to us (1:12; 3:11).

Similarly, the book of Hebrews was written because the enemy Satan utilized even Judaism, the religion ordained and appointed by God, to replace Christ. Judaism was ordained, appointed, established, and used by God. We may illustrate Judaism by a medicine bottle. A mother's intention may be to give medicine to her child, but the naughty child may care for the bottle, not the medicine. God's intention is not to work Judaism into His chosen people. His intention is to work Christ into His chosen people, but the enemy of God utilized Judaism to replace Christ and substitute for Him. That is why the writer of Hebrews wrote that book, telling us that Christ is above all and better than all. Christ, not Judaism or anything religious, is the goal.

Similarly, Galatians was written because at that time the

Judaizers were utilized by the enemy to make the law a substitute for Christ. The law was given by God, but even something given by God can be used by the enemy to replace Christ, to take the place of Christ among God's chosen people. Paul wrote the first Epistle to the Corinthians to adjust the Corinthians concerning teachings and the use of the gifts, including speaking in tongues. The enemy utilized even the New Testament dispensational gifts to replace Christ. In 1:22 and 23 Paul said, "For indeed Jews require signs and Greeks seek wisdom, but we preach Christ crucified." Even gifts, signs, and wisdom can be certain kinds of substitutes for Christ. All these things—philosophy, religion, law, and gifts—were substitutes for Christ in the first century of the church.

Then from the second century down to the present time there have been many other substitutes. Forms, teachings, and many other things have substituted for Christ. Many people, for example, stand not for Christ alone but for a certain kind of teaching. Roman Catholicism itself is a great and evil substitute for Christ. Even theology substitutes for God; the -*ology*, the study, substitutes for *Theos*, the reality. The enemy is subtle to use something that is very close to but not the real item. He injects it into us, and we are poisoned by it without being aware of it. Unconsciously we are distracted by something which is very close to Christ. Today in the so-called Christian churches there are choirs and solos, and there are also certain sinful things. There are all kinds of substitutes—good, evil, spiritual, and secular. Satan does not care what kind of substitute it is; as long as he can distract us from Christ, that is good enough for him.

The System of Clergy and Laity

The second category of Satan's frustrations and damage to the church is the system of the clergy. According to history, Satan not only used many substitutes to replace and usurp the place of Christ, but he also invented the clerical system. Today there is a difference between the clergy and laity. This kills the functions of the members of the Body of Christ. Originally all the members of the Body, without exception, were functioning, but gradually the enemy set up the system of the clergy to limit the function to a small number of believers while the majority of believers were put out of their function. In this way the Body became paralyzed. This is the subtlety of the enemy. Satan's first frustration is to kill the life of the Body, which is Christ, by substituting many other things for Christ. The second frustration is that the enemy invented the system of the clergy.

Divisions in the Body of Christ

Satan is not satisfied to have only these two frustrations. The third item of his frustration and damage is divisions, sects, and denominations. These not only replace the life and kill the functions of the Body, but they cut the Body into pieces. In this way the expression of Christ is damaged. The life is replaced, the functions are damaged, and the whole Body is cut into pieces. There are many real Christians in a large city, perhaps at least fifty thousand genuine believers. If these fifty thousand real believers were not divided, they would have a great impact. It would be easy to conquer and subdue the whole United States.

The enemy is very subtle. He has replaced Christ by usurping His ground and place, killed the functions of the members, and divided the Body. How poor and pitiful this is! Many Christian are not related to one another. They are merely independent, isolated, individual believers. Because of this, there are many members, but we do not have the Body. The enemy is still doing this work today. He utilizes many good things to isolate us. The enemy works in our reasoning, but regardless of the reasons, as long as we are isolated, this is good enough for the enemy.

By the above three categories of means, Satan has almost completely damaged the church life. The United States is a nation of Christianity. The forefathers of this country came over to this land mostly because of their Christian faith. But today, even in this country, where is the church? We have substitutes for Christ, we have the clergy, and we have the divisions, but we do not have the church. There is no need to argue with this; the facts are apparent. The church has been damaged by these three categories of things. This is why in all these days we have stressed Christ as our life, content, and everything to us—not the substitutes for Christ, but Christ Himself. This is also why we help one another to function as members of the Body. We do not want to have either the clergy or the laity. Rather, we have the brothers and sisters as functioning members. We all have to function. If you say that I am a "pastor," I will say that you are a "minister." We encourage all the brothers and sisters to minister in order to express Christ. Why then do we pay so much attention to the ground of the church? It is to deal with the divisions.

FIGHTING THE BATTLE FOR THE LORD'S RECOVERY OF THE ONENESS OF THE CHURCH

The Lord's recovery today consists of three main items. It is the recovery of Christ as life and everything to us, the recovery of the universal priesthood with the functions of all the members, and the recovery of the proper oneness of the church. It is when these three items are recovered that we will have the proper and adequate church life. There must be a group of believers who take Christ as their unique life and content, who realize that each one of us must function not as clergy or laity but as living members, and who give up the divisions, sects, and denominations to come to the proper ground to practice the proper oneness. If there is a people like this, they will realize the Lord's recovery in a full way.

In some places certain dear friends have advised me, saying. "Praise the Lord, you have a ministry from the Lord. As long as you expound the Word, we appreciate it, but do not talk about the church." As I spoke in a certain city recently, my hosts treated me honorably, but they said, "Everyone appreciates your ministry about the inner life, but this is not the right time to touch the issue of the church." They did everything they could to stop me from speaking anything about the church, but on the last night I was there, I said, "I do not take care of this restriction. I have to speak something about the church." When I began to read from Romans 12 in order to say something about the Body, all those dear friends were grieved. The next morning when we were leaving, no one came to see us off. Praise the Lord, I like to be treated in this way! I like to suffer for the Body of Christ. Many dear friends in the Far East and Europe advised me in the same way, not only face to face but also in long writings. They said that the Lord's work among us is good, but the matter of the church is like dead flies that "cause the perfumer's ointment to stink" (Eccl. 10:1). I have the notorious title of being "the strongest exponent of the church in the Far East." I am not worthy to have this title. I am nobody and nothing, yet certain people have given me such a big title. This is the subtlety of the enemy. I praise the Lord that I am counted worthy to suffer in this way.

We published a book in Chinese by Brother Watchman Nee that originally was entitled *Holy without Blemish*. When we translated that book into English, we felt that the title should be changed to *The Glorious Church*. When the book was published as *Holy without Blemish,* it sold very well. Many people ordered it. However, when we changed the title to *The Glorious Church,* there were no further sales, even though it was the same book. This is because it spoke about the church. The church is the stumbling stone. Oh, how subtle the enemy is! We have to fight the battle for the church. The more I am advised not to speak about the church, the more I do speak about the church. The more someone tries to shut my mouth, the more I wish I had two mouths with which to speak.

PRACTICING THE BODY LIFE WITHOUT DIVISION

In a large city such as Los Angeles, there are many denominations and divisions. When someone is saved and becomes a member of the Body of Christ, he must live the Body life. How then can he realize the Body life? Should he place himself in the Roman Catholic Church? Should he go to the Presbyterians, Baptists, or Episcopalians? Where can he practice the Body life? This is a real problem; it is not a small matter. This is why we need to have the proper ground of the church without any denominational element, a ground without any division. The proper ground is the ground of the locality, the local ground, the unique ground of the oneness of the church.

The one who is saved should try his best to find other believers in his city, and he should meet with them, help them, and be helped by them. Then these believers, who are not in the denominations but simply living in this city, should come together not to form anything, not to create another division, but to stand on the ground of the locality where they are. If any others who are in the "small circles" of divisions realize that they have to give up the circles, they should do it. If they do not, however, there is no need to proselyte them. There are many unsaved ones to whom we can testify, minister Christ, bring to Christ, and bring into this proper church life. To practice in this way is to practice the unique ground of oneness.

If this brother one day moves to another city, he should first realize that he is simply a brother in that city. Then he should do his best to find others there who take the same standing of the local ground, the ground of oneness. When he meets with them, he should try to help them and try to be helped by them. These who come together become a group of believers standing on the proper ground in that city. If in that city there is already a group of believers standing on this proper ground, the brother has to be willing to submit himself to them. He should not say, "Those people seem peculiar to me. When I pray, I pray in a very silent way, but those people pray too emotionally. I do not want to join them. I will start another meeting in my home where I can pray silently." If he says this, he will eventually raise up a "praying silently" church. He may not declare or claim to be doing that; he may proclaim that he is not sectarian or denominational. In actuality, however, that is what he is doing. This is the problem with divisions. If the brother finds a group of genuine believers standing on the proper ground, then regardless of the way they have their meeting, practice their service, or pray, he has to join them.

To say this is easy, but within only the past two years we have been tested in this regard. Certain brothers heard about our meeting in Los Angeles and came to us imagining that we must be something in the third heavens. When they came, however, they realized that we were actually something in "the valley." They began to ask, "Why this?" and "Why that?" in a divisive way. As long as someone asks in this way, he is sectarian. The answer to "Why this?" is that we are simply the church in Los Angeles. The answer to "Why that?" is that we are, in principle, the church in Jerusalem or the church in Antioch. If someone does not care to meet with the church on the local ground, he should not raise up another meeting in this city. To do so would be sectarian. Someone may say, "These poor people in Los Angeles pray 'in the valley.' I want to meet where I can pray 'in the heavens.'" He may do so, but he should go to another city to do that. When he gets to that city, however, he may find that there is already a group of people standing on the proper ground. If he tries to move away to yet another city, he still must take the standing of the proper ground in that city. Eventually, he must submit himself, or he will create a division. We have no right to make a division.

THE UNIQUE CENTER FOR THE WORSHIP TO GOD

Someone may ask us, "If you have no right to make a division, then why do you not join our circle? Why do you separate yourselves from all the circles? Is that not a division?" We cannot join those "circles" because they are divisions. To join any one of them is to join a division. How can we do this? We must keep away from divisions. Consider the picture of Israel in the good land. When God brought all His people into the land, He chose Jerusalem as the unique place for them to come together to worship Him. According to Deuteronomy 12 through 16, Jerusalem was the one unique center. Verse 5 of chapter twelve says, "But to the place which Jehovah your God will choose out of all your tribes to put His name, to His habitation, shall you seek, and there shall you go." All the people of the twelve tribes had to come to this one place. No one had the right to set up another place of worship, regardless of the reason. It is by the unique center for worship that the oneness of the twelve tribes was constantly kept throughout all the centuries.

Suppose that the Israelites had the right to set up other centers for worship. After five years another small center may have been set up in the north, and after another five years, more centers may have been set up in other regions. By all these centers, the people of God eventually would have been divided. However, they were not allowed to do this. They had no right to do this. One Israelite may have fought with his neighbor just before the Feast of Tabernacles. When the time of the feast came, however, both he and his neighbor, as males of the people of Israel, had no other choice but to go to Jerusalem. If one saw the other on the way to Jerusalem, he had no right to say, "Are you going there? Then I will not. I will set up a center for worship right here." If he did this, he would be cut off from the people of Israel. To be cut off was to suffer death. This was very serious. All the males of the people of Israel had to go to the one unique place three times a year. In order not to be cut off, each one had to go to the same place, even if his enemy was there. Not only did they have to go to that place; they also had to worship God by offering the peace offering and sharing it with one another. This would compel each one to say, "Brother, forgive me." Then they would experience Psalm 133: "Behold, how good and how pleasant it is / For brothers to dwell in unity!" (v. 1).

According to Deuteronomy 12 through 16, there was no possibility to have division. There was no alternative, no choice. They were bound and limited. God already had chosen a place for them to go, and they had no right to choose for themselves. Ninety percent of the produce that they reaped from the good land they could enjoy in any place of their choice at any time. However, they had no right to choose the place to enjoy the tithe of ten percent. To enjoy that portion of the rich surplus of the land, they had to go to the only place chosen and appointed by God. This is a type of our experience today. On the one hand, we have the right to enjoy and experience Christ at any time and in any place that we like. However, as long as we are going to have the church life to enjoy Christ in a corporate way as a worship to the Father, we have no choice. We have to do this to keep the oneness of the Body.

A REMNANT RETURNING TO SEPARATE THEMSELVES FOR THE ONENESS, BUT NOT TO MAKE A DIVISION

The people of Israel did as God commanded, but once they were captured, they went into exile in Babylon and other places for seventy years. After the seventy years, the Lord came in to call them to come back to keep the oneness. However, not all the people in exile came back; only a small number, a minority, returned. When this small number returned to the place of oneness, spontaneously they separated themselves from those who did not return. This was a separation, but it was not a division. They simply came back to realize the proper oneness on the proper ground. It was those who still insisted on remaining in Babylon who made the division. Those who came back had the oneness, but those who remained in exile kept the divisions.

Someone who remained in the exile might have said, "Ezra and Nehemiah, you preach that we have to keep the oneness of the people of the Lord. Why then do you separate from us? Why do you not stay with us and join us? On the one hand, you preach oneness, but on the other hand, you create division." If someone asks us in this way, we should say, "Brother, come along with me. We can keep the oneness only on the proper ground. As long as you are outside the proper ground, you are in division. Therefore, it is not lawful for me to join you. If I join you, I join the division."

Someone may ask, "What about Daniel? Daniel remained in Babylon and did not return from exile." It is true that under the Lord's sovereignty Daniel did not go back. Still, Daniel's heart and his eyes were always going back. Day by day he opened his window and prayed toward Jerusalem (Dan. 6:10). We should not take Daniel's case as an excuse not to return to the oneness. It is not right to stay back. We cannot have the real oneness on the wrong ground. We have to come back to the proper ground. We cannot have real oneness in a denomination. To join a denomination is to join a division.

Some Israelites left Babylon, but they stopped midway in the Arab lands before they reached the proper ground. In doing this, they created another division. Others who left Babylon came back to places very close to Jerusalem, but they stopped short. This created yet another division. We have to come back to the unique ground, the ground of oneness, the local ground. Some may say, "We have given up the denominations. We now have free groups in our homes." However, that ground may be in "the Arab lands" or even close to Jerusalem, but it is not yet the proper ground. It is still in division.

In the present day, the nation of Israel has only a few million people. In New York, however, there are even more millions of Jews. Who are the ones in division, those who went back to Palestine to form the nation of Israel or those who are in New York? It is those who remain in New York, simply because they are on the wrong ground. If they want to practice the Jewish oneness, they have to go back to Israel. They can never practice the proper oneness in New York. New York is a ground for division, not for oneness.

We may also use the illustration of a university with several thousand students. The school may call all the students to be assembled in the auditorium. Most of the students, however, may not like to go there. Some would prefer to assemble in another hall, some in a dormitory, some in their small rooms, and some outside. They all have their own choice and taste, and most of them would not follow the rule of the school. Only a small number, perhaps twenty or thirty, may consider that since they are students of this school, they have to take the order of the school and assemble in the proper place. Then they would call the others and say, "Friends, let us come together." Who are the ones taking the proper ground, and who are taking the wrong ground? All the other assemblies are wrong; they are divisions. Only a small number of students are endeavoring to keep the oneness of the school. One of the other meetings may have twenty thousand students, but they are still a division because their ground is wrong. We have to keep the oneness on the proper ground.

CLOSING THE BACK DOOR TO DIVISIONS

As human beings, we have to be Christians. To be a

Christian is to be a member of the Body. As members of the Body, we must have the Body life, and to be in the Body life, we must find the proper ground, put ourselves on it, and practice the proper church life. This is very important; it is not a small matter. Without the proper ground there is no safeguard against further divisions. If we do not realize the proper ground, we may be happy today, but after two months we may all feel unhappy. We may start another meeting in another place and feel that there is no difference between the two places of meetings. Then after five months someone may start a third place of meeting. This can go on endlessly if there is no safeguard, standard, or limitation. However, if we all realize the proper ground and have the vision, the light, concerning the church ground, we will be limited. The back door for divisions will be closed. No one among us could make any divisions because we know that in order to have the oneness in the church life, we must keep ourselves on the proper ground.

TURNING TO THE GENTILES WITH FAITH AND A VISION OF THE PROPER ONENESS

We cannot remain in the denominations, because they are divisions. However, if someone desires to stay in the denominations, there is no need to argue with him or to try to convince him to come out. Many times both in the Far East and in the Western world, Christians came to me and said, "Brother Lee, I do not feel that it is necessary for me to give up the denominations." I said to them, "Brothers, do what you feel in peace." If they want to stay there, let them, but eventually they will suffer a loss.

Some may think that we should go to the denominations and fellowship with them so that they can see what we have. We have done this many times. In 1937 I traveled throughout almost all the northern provinces of China for this purpose, but very little resulted from that. In Acts 13 the apostles did their best to minister the word to the Jews, but the Jews rejected it. The apostle then said, "Behold, we turn to the Gentiles" (v. 46). If we are rejected, we should do the same thing. I can never forget how in May of 1934 Brother

Nee and I talked together as we drove from Shanghai to a little city nearby. While he was driving, he turned to me and said, "Brother Lee, now we have no other way but to turn to the Gentiles." He said this because at that time we were rejected by Christianity in China. People used our writings on the gospel, edification, and life, but in one matter—the church—they could not get through. We were rejected because of this. People came to us secretly to buy our books; they liked those books and they used them, but they would not take the way of the church. Therefore, Brother Nee was forced and compelled to say, "Let us go to the Gentiles."

We praise the Lord that after a few years the work began in a prevailing way among the Gentiles. A good number were brought into the church life. Hundreds of new converts were baptized daily. Our success depends on how faithful we are to the Lord. Do not look at the environment, at the present situation. We must have faith, and we must have the vision.

CHAPTER THREE

THE CHRISTIAN MEETINGS AS A TESTIMONY OF THE ENJOYMENT OF CHRIST IN OUR DAILY LIFE

Scripture Reading: 2 Tim. 4:22; Gal. 6:18; Philem. 25; 1 Cor. 6:17; John 4:21-24; Deut. 16:16

The Christian meeting, that is, the way to meet together, is a very common matter to Christians. In this message, however, we will see something that is not common. What is the proper way for Christians to have their meetings, and where can we find some instruction in the New Testament that tells us how to have our meetings? Is the way of meeting which Christianity takes today the right way? Is the way of meeting which we take the right way?

It seems that 1 Corinthians 14:26 is the only portion of the Word in which we can find instruction on how to have our meetings. As far as I can tell from the history of the church, this verse was discovered by the Brethren in the nineteenth century. The Brethren were raised up around 1828. Not long after that, according to what we can read from their writings, they received light on 1 Corinthians 14:26. From that time on, the Brethren insisted very much that whenever Christians come together, it should not be in the way of a pastor or minister teaching and bearing the full responsibility of the meeting. Rather, all the brothers had to share the responsibility of the meeting, following the Holy Spirit to share something with the others.

However, after many years of experiences I came to the conclusion that even in this verse we do not have the proper way to have our meeting. This verse is more or less on the technical side, giving us some techniques, but strictly speaking, it does not give us the way. What then is the way? It seems we do not have any such instructions. There is nothing in the book of Acts that tells us the way. In the Epistles, Ephesians 5:19 tells us to sing psalms, hymns, and spiritual songs. However, this refers more to the Christian daily life. Even though this verse tells us to speak to one another, it is not clear that it refers to the meetings. Therefore, strictly speaking, it is hard to find any passage in the New Testament giving us an instruction for the way to have our meetings.

Is the way of meeting which Christianity takes today the right way? We can quickly answer "no." We must drop the way of Christianity. It is abnormal, religious, and altogether derived from tradition, and we must give it up. What about our way of meeting today? We also have to admit that our way is not the right way, because we came from the religious way. We have been too much influenced by our background. This is not only the case today. Thirty years ago I personally listened to Brother Watchman Nee talk about this matter. At that time he was trying to do away with the message meeting on the Lord's Day morning. He challenged us, asking, "What kind of meeting is this?" Yes, we called the Lord's Day morning meeting the message meeting or the edification meeting, but he said that this meeting was merely according to the traditional way, for church goers to have a religious "service." He said that there is no scriptural ground for this kind of meeting, so we should drop it. This has been taught for more than thirty years, but still today we have not yet dropped this way of meeting. Oh, we do not know how much we have been influenced by tradition and our background!

THE CHRISTIAN MEETING BEING A CORPORATE EXPRESSION OF OUR DAILY LIFE

Before we can find the way to have our meeting, we have to know what the Christian meeting is. The Christian meeting is a corporate expression of our Christian life. In other words, it is an expression of the Christian life, in a corporate way. We all agree that the most important meeting for us is the Lord's table meeting. We Christians may give up any kind of meeting, but one meeting we should not give up is the meeting for the Lord's table. Why do we come together to have the Lord's table? Someone may say that it is simply to remember the Lord. If we understand the meaning of the Lord's table only to this extent, our understanding is still religious. The Lord's table is a testimony, a declaration, a proclamation, in a corporate way of the Christian life. We live and we walk by the crucified, resurrected, and ascended Christ. He is our life, and we live by Him day by day. Now once a week on the first day of the week, on the day of His resurrection, we come together to testify of this kind of life, to make a declaration, a proclamation, and a testimony in a corporate way to the whole universe that we live by the crucified, resurrected, and ascended Christ. By this we can understand that the meeting is the corporate testimony of our individual daily lives.

The prayer meeting is also a testimony, an expression, in a corporate way of the Christian prayer life. If all the brothers and sisters did not pray in their daily life, we could not come together to have a good prayer meeting. If we have a proper life of prayer individually, then we can have a proper prayer meeting corporately. By this again, we can see that the Christian meeting is a corporate expression of the Christian life.

This is also true of the meeting for studying the Word. If none of us studied the Word in our daily life, then when we came together to study the Word, we would have to ask a professor or seminary graduate to teach us the Word. This is not a proper study meeting. The proper meeting to study the Word of God must be a corporate expression of the individual Christian life of studying. I study the Word, you study the Word, and every one studies the Word in his or her daily life. Then we all come together to have a corporate expression of our study life.

Similarly, if none of us cares for sinners and does not preach the gospel, who will preach the gospel when we come together for a gospel meeting? In our daily life and walk, we all should preach the gospel and be the Lord's witnesses to people. Then we may feel the need for a certain day to come together to have a corporate expression of this kind of life. This is the gospel preaching meeting. Again we see that the Christian meeting is a corporate expression of the Christian life.

The testimony meeting is the same. If we never testify for the Lord, then when we come together, we will all come with our mouths shut. Then whom shall we ask to give a testimony? The testimony meeting is an expression in a corporate way of the Christian life of testifying. The meeting for fellowship is also in this manner. If we do not fellowship with one another, how can we come together to have fellowship? By all these examples, we can discover the principle for the Christian meeting. The Christian meeting is the corporate expression of the Christian life.

EXPERIENCING CHRIST BY EXERCISING OUR SPIRIT

The way to have our Christian life is to exercise our spirit to constantly experience Christ in our spirit. By *spirit* we do not simply mean the Holy Spirit. Rather, day by day we have to experience Christ in our human spirit. This is the way of the Christian life. To emphasize our human spirit may be compared to teaching small children the way to eat. A small child may not put food in his mouth properly. He may even put the food on his nose. It seems that he does not even know what the mouth is and where it is. Therefore, we may be forced and compelled to tell him, "That is not the right way to eat. You have to eat with your mouth." To say this is not to be dogmatic; it is very necessary. If a child does not know the proper way to eat and the proper organ to use, he will be weak. It is the same with exercising our spirit in our daily life.

In the New Testament we cannot find a word telling us to live and walk in the heart, the soul, or the mind. Yes, we have to love the Lord with our heart and be renewed in our mind, but we are never told to walk in the mind or live by the mind. Rather, the New Testament many times tells us to walk in the spirit and live in the spirit. This does not refer simply to the Holy Spirit. Second Timothy 4:22 says, "The Lord be with your spirit," using the word *your*. The Christian life is a life of experiencing Christ, but where is Christ for us to experience? There is no ground for anyone to argue; the Word says clearly that Christ is "with your spirit." Therefore, we all have to learn how to experience Christ by our spirit.

Galatians 6:18 says, "The grace of our Lord Jesus Christ be with your spirit." The last verse of the book of Philemon says the same thing: "The grace of the Lord Jesus Christ be with your spirit" (v. 25). The grace of the Lord is the Lord Himself enjoyed by us. Therefore, the Christian life is a life of experiencing Christ in our spirit. Day by day we experience Christ in our spirit, and day by day we live in our spirit and learn how to walk in the spirit. Our spirit is where the Holy Spirit dwells, and it is one spirit with the Lord as the Spirit (2 Cor. 3:17). First Corinthians 6:17 says, "But he who is joined to the Lord is one spirit." Day by day we walk in this spirit and we live in this spirit to experience Christ and contact Christ. This is our life. What is the Christian life? The Christian life is a life of experiencing Christ by the spirit.

How much Christ do we have in our Christian life? How much exercise of the spirit do we have? We may have many other good things, such as patience. In fact, we have more patience than we have Christ. We may also have more sincerity than Christ. This means that at least some of our sincerity is not Christ. It is hard for us to tell lies; we are honest, but we may have more honesty than we have Christ. This indicates that a certain part of the brothers' and sisters' good life is not Christ. It is too much by the self, that is, by the soul, not by the exercise of our spirit, that we have sincerity and honesty. If I have much sincerity by my self, you have honesty by your self, the sisters have meekness and humility by their self, and we all have many good attributes by our self, when we come together to meet, what kind of meeting will we have? We will have self-realization and not genuine fellowship.

A sister may be very meek, gentle, and nice, just like the statue of Mary in front of a Catholic cathedral. Another sister may be very humble, and many brothers may be sincere, faithful, and honest. Then when all these peculiar self-realizing people come together, they will have a peculiar self-realizing Christian meeting. In the nineteenth century the Brethren discovered 1 Corinthians 14:26, and they passed this discovery on to many wonderful but self-realizing

Christians. Today, everyone comes to the meeting simply to sit there in his meek, humble, and sincere way. The more each one sits there, the more he becomes a "tomb" and the more the whole meeting becomes a "cemetery," very quiet, with everything in decent order. This is due to the lack of a proper Christian life.

If we realize that to have a proper Christian life we must daily experience Christ, we will not care about our honesty and meekness. Rather, we will truly care for Christ. We will care to exercise to contact the Lord. We will exercise the spirit and live in the spirit. Morning and evening, day and night, we will have real fellowship with the Lord in the spirit. Then we will constantly have many experiences of Christ as our meekness, Christ as our sincerity, and Christ as our everything. We will be strong, living, active, and positive in our spirit. Our inner man will be strengthened and full of the experience of Christ. Then we can come to the meeting full of Christ, with the full, rich experiences of Christ and with a strong, living, active, and positive spirit. If we all come to the meeting in such a way, we will spontaneously exercise the spirit and minister Christ. This is the right way to have a meeting.

MEETING BY BRINGING THE SURPLUS
OF THE GOOD LAND AS AN OFFERING TO GOD

It is hard to find a passage in the Word with this kind of instruction. However, if we do know the Old and New Testaments and have some amount of revelation from the Lord, we will realize that this is something that is revealed in the Scriptures. The worship mentioned in John 4, when the Samaritan woman spoke with the Lord, is not the individual worship but the corporate worship. It is the worship in the meeting. In ancient times, all the males of the people of God had to meet three times a year—at the Feast of Unleavened Bread, at the Feast of Weeks (that is, at Pentecost), and at the Feast of Tabernacles (Deut. 16:16). The way they met was to bring the surplus of the good land and to offer this surplus as a worship to God. This surplus was a kind of symbol, a representation, of their life. They all lived on the good land and labored on the good land, from the beginning to the end of the year. They tilled the ground, sowed the seed, and watered the plants. Then they had a harvest to reap, and they lived on what they reaped from their labor on the good land. Then from that harvest which they reaped, they put aside a part for their worship together.

The good land typifies Christ. We have been saved by God and brought into Christ. We have been put into Christ as our good land. Therefore, we have to labor on Him day by day to have something to reap, and we live on what we reap of Christ. Then we can come together with what we live on. This is the proper experience of Christ.

Whenever all of Israel came together, they came with a certain amount of the surplus of their produce to offer to the Lord. They offered some as the burnt offering, some as the meal offering, some as the peace offering, some as the sin offering, and some as the trespass offering. Some they offered in the eyes of God as the wave offering and the heave offering. All that they brought to the Lord as an offering, they brought from the produce of the good land. A part of what they offered was burnt to be food to God, as a sweet smelling savor for His enjoyment. The rest, however, they enjoyed with one another. If at that time we could have been in that meeting, we would have seen an exhibition of all the rich produce, the surplus, of the good land. God enjoyed those offerings, and all the worshippers also enjoyed those offerings with God, in the presence of God, and with one another. This was their way of meeting.

In John 4, the Samaritan woman raised up the question of worship (v. 20). The Lord Jesus told her, "An hour is coming when neither in this mountain nor in Jerusalem will you worship the Father" (v. 21). *An hour is coming* means the dispensation had changed. Now it is the hour for God's people to worship, not by going to Jerusalem and not with the offerings as types, but to worship in spirit and truthfulness (v. 24). Our worship today is not with the offerings but with the reality, who is Christ. Today we have to labor on Christ. We must reap many riches of Christ for us to live on and to have a surplus to bring to the meeting for worship to God.

The way for the people of God to meet together is to bring

the surplus of Christ to the meeting to offer to God by exercising our spirit. Day by day we labor on our good land, which is Christ. Then we have some real experiences of Christ to reap. We live on all that we reap of Christ, and we have a surplus of what we have reaped to bring to the meeting. Then in the meeting we offer what we have experienced of Christ to God for His satisfaction and for our enjoyment in the presence of God with one another. This is the way for us to meet.

LEAVING OUR TRADITION AND OLD CONCEPTS TO COME TO THE MEETING IN A LIVING WAY WITH THE CHRIST WE HAVE ENJOYED

Concerning the technique for meeting, there are no rules or regulations. Regardless of what kind of meeting we have—for the Lord's table, for prayer, for study, or for a message—we almost always sit and wait for a hymn. There is no such teaching that we should always start the meeting with a hymn. From where did we learn this? This is simply a tradition that has crept in. Whether starting with a hymn is right or wrong depends on Christ and the Spirit. Moreover, from whom did we learn that only the responsible brothers should announce a hymn? Who gave us this kind of regulation? We should not condemn the responsible brothers for this, because it is we who have been too much of a "tomb." Because we do not take the responsibility, the so-called responsible brothers are forced to act as the "clergy." We may say that we do not have a laity and a clergy, but in actuality we do. Each of us is responsible for this. May the Lord be merciful to us.

We have to change our concept. Our old concept must be dropped. This is not a matter merely of changing the forms. This is a matter that depends on our daily life. We all have to live by Christ. We all have to labor on the good land, and we have to exercise our spirit. Then when we come to the meeting, there is no need to wait. There is no need to have either a prayer or a hymn first. Everything will come out spontaneously. The right way to meet requires that we have a proper daily walk, have an adequate experience of Christ, and exercise our spirit. Then our spirit will be strengthened, living, active, and positive. Then when we come to the meeting, we will spontaneously pray.

Some may say that this spontaneous way will cause confusion. I do not believe it will, but I would even prefer this kind of living "confusion" to a deadened order. If we all live in the spirit to experience Christ, whatever we pray when we come to the meeting will be right. Variety will produce beauty. If we could go to the feasts of the people of Israel, we would see the variety of the riches of the surplus. If we all pray from our experience of Christ by exercising our spirit, even if there is a variety, there will still be the beauty, and there will be the flow of life.

Because we have been influenced by certain kinds of regulations, each one comes just to sit here. We are used to doing this. I am not saying that we need a change of form. Rather, we need a change in life and a change of concept. Then we will be truly diligent, zealous, active, positive, strong, and living in the spirit. As Christian brothers and sisters, we have to conduct our Christian life in this way, day by day laboring on Christ and experiencing Him by our spirit. We must learn how to exercise our spirit, be strengthened, be living, and be active and positive in our spirit to experience Christ all the time.

Then whenever we come to the meeting, we must realize that it is our duty to share something. Deuteronomy 16:16 tells us that the people of God could not appear before Jehovah empty-handed. They had to come to the feast with something of the good land. Likewise, we need to have something of Christ to bring to the meeting. Then we all will be open to Him, and there will be a way widely opened for the Holy Spirit to move among us. Many riches of Christ will come out and be offered to God for His satisfaction and for our enjoyment in the presence of God with one another. This is our way of meeting and our worship to God. In this way there will be no forms, regulations, laity, or clergy. Rather, all the living members will bring something of Christ to offer to God by the exercise of the spirit. This is the proper way to meet.

We are on the way of recovery, and this way to meet is an item in the Lord's recovery. We have to drop the old way, the way of form and regulation taken from the tradition we formerly practiced. Let us look to the Lord and cooperate with Him. I say again, we should not merely change our form, but we must change our realization, our concept, and our way of life. Then we will come to the meeting in the living way, with a new way of life under a new realization.

COMING TO THE MEETINGS WITH A LIVING SPIRIT

Because most of us came from the background of traditional Christianity, and we still have that environment surrounding us, it is very hard to change our concept concerning the meetings. In the past we have preached the gospel in a living way to people who were one hundred percent Gentiles. They never had any connection or relationship with a so-called Christian church. When they were saved, we simply gave them a little word, and they all knew how to function. For many old Christians, though, it is very hard to function, because they have too much influence from their background. We must try our best to drop our backgrounds and learn to live and walk in the spirit by enjoying and experiencing Christ in a practical way. Day by day we enjoy Christ, and day by day we experience Him in the spirit. Then whenever we come together, we come with a living, satisfied, refreshed, strengthened, uplifted, positive, and active spirit and with a certain amount of the experience of Christ.

When we come to a meeting, we should not consider what kind of meeting it is. Rather, we must consider it as a chance to worship, to share our burden, and to do our duty. We should forget our considerations and simply come to meet with one another as Christians. This is a matter of whether or not we are in the spirit, whether or not we are praying in the spirit with something of Christ. If we share something of Christ from the spirit, any portion is good. That will never disturb the meeting. As long as we exercise our spirit to express and minister something of Christ, that is right. That will release others' spirits, bring in the flow, and spontaneously begin the meeting.

Perhaps we will not sing a hymn at the beginning of the meeting. The brothers and sisters may simply pray. It may be, though, that we sing hymn after hymn. We should have no regulation, only the flow. However, this flow absolutely depends on a living spirit. Our spirit must be living. When our spirit is dead and we are poor with Christ, having nothing of Christ, whatever we do will be wrong. Even if everyone opens his mouth, that still will be wrong. In fact, the more we open our mouth, the more we will have a stinking odor, not the odor of a sweet fragrance. Whatever we do must be something living that comes from within.

Someone may ask, "What if I am fallen and have a failure the day of the meeting?" We have not only the burnt offering, the meal offering, and the peace offering. We also have the trespass offering. If we have a failure, we should come to the meeting with a contrite spirit to repent and confess before the Lord. We can exercise our contrite spirit to offer a prayer to the Lord for confession, repenting and applying the cleansing of the blood of Jesus. Even this kind of prayer will bring a flow into the meeting, because it is something living, something of Christ, and a real experience of Christ as the trespass offering. Perhaps then the flow will bring in many prayers of appreciation to Christ as the trespass offering. Many may follow to pray, "Lord, we do thank You that we have the experience of You being our trespass offering." That will be something living in the flow.

We must prepare ourselves to come to the meeting. I have a deep sense that we need to change our concept and change our way of life. This will help us to be diligent and fervent in the spirit in our daily walk. Then we can come to the meeting in a new way. Someone may say that not meeting in the traditional way will cause confusion. Whether or not releasing our spirit will cause confusion is yet to be seen. Let us try it. If it causes confusion, we can try something else. Let us go on and see what we find and what will come out of it. Please be at peace; I can assure you that we will not suffer a loss by exercising our spirit in the meetings.

I am not suggesting that we change a form or regulation. That never works. Rather, we have to change our concept and realization. We have to change the way of our Christian living. We have to learn how to live and walk in and by Christ by exercising our spirit. Our realization and concept must change, and our way of living must be different. Then when we come together, spontaneously we will have something of Christ.

CHAPTER FOUR

FOUR MAIN ITEMS
IN THE LORD'S TABLE MEETING

Scripture Reading: 1 Cor. 10:21; 11:23-25; 1 Cor. 15:45b; John 4:24; 1 John 2:23; Heb. 2:11b-12; Matt. 26:30

REMEMBERING THE LORD BEING TO PARTAKE OF HIM

There are four main items that we must practice in the Lord's table meeting. First, to remember the Lord at His table is to partake of Him. The biblical ground for this is in 1 Corinthians 10 and 11. Verses 23 through 25 of chapter eleven say, "For I received from the Lord that which also I delivered to you, that the Lord Jesus in the night in which He was betrayed took bread, and having given thanks, He broke it and said, This is My body, which is given for you; this do unto the remembrance of Me. Similarly also the cup after they had dined, saying, This cup is the new covenant established in My blood; this do, as often as you drink it, unto the remembrance of Me." This indicates that to remember the Lord in a real way is to take, eat, and drink of Him.

To eat and to drink something is to partake of it. Verse 21 of chapter ten says, "You cannot drink the Lord's cup and the demons' cup; you cannot partake of the Lord's table and of the demons' table." It is not our own word to say that we partake of the Lord; in the Bible we have this phrase: *partake of the Lord's table*. Since this is a table, it must be something for us to enjoy. In 1 Corinthians 11 there is eating and drinking, and in chapter ten there is the table and the partaker of the table. All of this strongly proves that to remember the Lord, to have the Lord's table, is to partake of the Lord. When we come to the Lord's table, we do not merely remember Him in our mind. Rather, we partake of the Lord, enjoy Him once again, eat and drink of Him, and sit at His table with the saints to share Him one with another. This is the first meaning of the Lord's table.

This thought, concept, and understanding is very much neglected by today's Christianity. Today when many Christians come to the so-called holy communion, they have the thought that they must remember what Jesus did for us, that He was the Son of God, and that He died on the cross for us. However, when we come to the table, we come again to take something of the Lord Himself. We come to partake of the Lord. The Lord's table is a table with the Lord Himself spread as a feast on the table. He has given Himself to us by His death and resurrection. Now He offers us not His blood first but His body. That His body is first and His blood follows proves that He is offering us Himself in resurrection. Even though the Lord set up the table before His death, it was something done in anticipation of His resurrection. He has given Himself to us by His death, and He has put Himself before us in His resurrection. Now in His resurrection we come to His table to enjoy Him, feast on Him, and eat and drink of Him.

PREPARING OURSELVES BY EXERCISING OUR SPIRIT

The second main point concerning the Lord's table is the exercise of our spirit. The way we come to the Lord's table to partake of the Lord, that is, to eat and drink of the Lord, is by exercising our spirit. If we do not know how to exercise our spirit, we cannot enjoy the Lord. This matter is neglected too much. Whenever we come to the Lord's table, we have to realize that we have come to partake of the Lord. Therefore, we need to exercise. Before we come to a delicious feast, we have to get ourselves ready. Many times when I was invited to a dinner, I asked the one inviting me what he would serve. If it is something that I truly desire, I prepare my appetite all day long for the coming dinner. Then I am able to go and enjoy it adequately. To come to the Lord's table is to partake of the Lord, to enjoy the Lord, to eat and drink something of the Lord. For this we have to prepare our spirit. Therefore, the second main item concerning this meeting is the exercise of the spirit.

Whenever we come to the Lord's table, we must realize that we are coming to enjoy the Lord. Today the Lord is the life-giving Spirit (1 Cor. 15:45b), and the way He imparts Himself to us is in our spirit. Therefore, we have to exercise our spirit. The strongest ground to prove this from the Bible is John 4 and 6. Verse 63 of chapter six says, "It is the Spirit who gives life; the flesh profits nothing; the words which I have spoken to you are spirit and are life." To this we can add John 4:24: "God is Spirit, and those who worship Him [that is, contact Him, enjoy Him, and partake of Him] must worship in spirit and truthfulness." We need to exercise our spirit.

We also need to give up all the preoccupying things. This means that we must not only prepare our spirit, but we have to open our spirit deeply. To open ourselves from our very depths is not only to open our mind and heart but to open our spirit. Whenever we come to the table, we have to prepare ourselves by opening to the Lord from our spirit, from the very depths of our being. It is not only that our sins have been purged away and that we have rid ourselves of the worldly things. It is also that we drop anything that preoccupies us, and we open deeply from within to the Lord. Then our spirit will be prepared and exercised.

SENSING THE ATMOSPHERE IN THE MEETING AND FOLLOWING THE FLOW OF THE SPIRIT

First, we must realize that we are coming to partake of the Lord. Then second, we need to get our spirit ready and exercised. The third practical matter concerning the Lord's table is even more important. We also have to sense the atmosphere of the meeting and follow the flow. These matters are very strategic. In order to have a good meeting for the Lord's table, we must have all these main items.

We may compare following the flow in the meeting to serving a feast, which requires that we know the proper way to serve. If we are to serve steak as the main dish, we must serve the steak first. We cannot serve ice cream as the first course in a feast of steak. We must know what the first course is and that the second course follows the first. Then we can have a proper feast in its proper courses. When we come to the Lord's table, we have to sense the atmosphere of the meeting and follow the flow. In that meeting will we "serve steak," or will we "serve fish"? We can, for example, stress what the Lord is, or we may stress the ascension and glory of the Lord.

In the meeting there is always a flow. We may illustrate the flow with a team playing a game. In basketball, the five members of the one team do not play with more than one ball; they play with only one ball. In this sense, the ball follows a flow, as in a stream. If one person in a basketball game plays with a football, and others play with many different kinds of balls, that game will be a mess. In the best games, all the members play with one ball in one flow. For this we need practice.

Although it seems that there is not much wrong with our Lord's table meeting, the tide of the Spirit is sometimes too low. This is due to the lack of the exercise of our spirit. Our spirit is not very living and strong. This may be due to the fact that we are afraid to make mistakes, but that still chokes us and quenches the Spirit.

Sometimes certain hymns frustrate the flow of prayer very much. At the beginning of the meeting there may be a real flow of prayer which is not fully expressed. This is not the right time to announce a hymn. Any hymn at such a time becomes a frustration to the flow of more prayers in the spirit. At other times, the worship to the Father may be the best portion of the meeting, but just when we come to the highest tide, a certain hymn again can frustrate the flow. Such a hymn can be like cold water poured on the fire. Just as we have the real sense that two or three more prayers will bring us to a climax, our mouths can be shut by the wrong hymn. To call a hymn in this way is the result of our forms, rituals, and knowledge. Therefore, we have to learn to sense the flow. We have to forget about mere knowledge. First we must sense the flow, and then we should exercise our proper knowledge to do things in an adequate, proper way. When there is a real flow of prayer, we should not do anything to frustrate it.

Sometimes we need a hymn to stir up the praying spirit. At other times, though, we should not call a hymn because the praying spirit is already present. To announce a hymn will stop the praying spirit. We have to follow the flow and not pay much attention to mere knowledge. To always say that after four or five prayers a hymn is needed to match the prayers is to act according to mere knowledge. The knowledge of the letter kills. We must pay attention to the flow. If there is a living flow, do not hinder it. Give the flow a free way to go on. We must learn to exercise the spirit to release something from within, and we must learn to always exercise the inner sense to take care of the flow.

THE WORSHIP TO THE FATHER

The fourth main point concerning the Lord's table is the worship to the Father. The Holy Spirit always brings people to Christ, the Son. When we are inspired by the Holy Spirit, we say, "Jesus is Lord!" (1 Cor. 12:3). In the same way, the Son always brings people to the Father. If you have the Son, then you have the Father. First John 2:23 says, "He who confesses the Son has the Father also." The principle here is that when we are touched by the Holy Spirit, we realize something of Christ, the Son, and when we experience the Son, He brings us to the Father. Therefore, after we have experienced the Lord at His table, we should not close the meeting. According to the principle, when we have experienced the Son, He brings us to the Father. It is not right to close the Lord's table meeting without coming to the Father.

Hebrews 2:11b and 12 say, "He is not ashamed to call them brothers, saying, 'I will declare Your name to My brothers; in the midst of the church I will sing hymns of praise to You.'" When does the Lord Jesus praise the Father in the church? It must be after the saints in the church have had the Lord's table. After we have experienced the Lord, the Son brings us to the Father to praise the Father in the midst of His brothers. Matthew 26:30 tells us that after the Lord established His table, He came to the Father to contact the Father by singing a hymn with the disciples. This is the principle to follow. Whenever we enjoy the Lord, we have to be brought to the Father through the Lord. This is why after we enjoy the table, we have to follow the Lord to worship the Father. The first part of the table meeting is to remember the Lord by partaking of Him. After partaking of the Lord, then the second part of the meeting is a time to worship the Father, following the Lord as the firstborn Son. We are the many sons following Him to worship the Father.

All these four main points are mostly neglected in today's Christianity. Neither the Catholic Church nor the so-called reformed churches pay attention to these matters when they have the "holy communion." If we are going to have the Lord's table, we must learn these four main items. We come to the table to partake of something of the Lord Himself. Therefore, we have to prepare our spirit, to cleanse ourselves, and to exercise the spirit to contact the Lord and enjoy Him. Then we learn the technique of how to sense the present atmosphere of the meeting and follow the flow in the meeting. If we all act as one "team," we will enjoy the Lord adequately and properly. Out of this enjoyment in the spirit, we have the Son. Then the Lord as the Son of the Father leads us to the Father, and we follow Him to worship the Father. In this way we will have a full meeting in two parts for two purposes: to remember the Lord and partake of Him, and to worship and praise the Father.

Chapter Five

PRACTICAL POINTS CONCERNING THE LORD'S TABLE MEETING

COMING ON TIME TO THE TABLE MEETING

Often the attendants at the Lord's table meeting do not come on time. At the start of the meeting, perhaps only one-third of the attendants are there; then gradually some more come. It may be twenty or thirty minutes later that all the saints have gradually come. This spoils the meeting very much. Suppose that five persons play in a basketball game. The first one comes to play by himself. Later another one comes, and after five minutes or more the third, fourth, and fifth ones come. What kind of game would that be? Suppose again that someone invites twenty people to attend a feast. First eight come, then six more, and then gradually the rest come. The food will be spoiled by that time.

We put so much stress on the Lord's table meeting because it is very important and means very much for the church life. In order for the church to be strong, we must have a proper meeting for the Lord's table. Therefore, we have to endeavor by the Lord's grace to start the table meeting with all the members present. We should have a feeling of shame whenever we come late to the Lord's table. It is a real shame to come late. If someone invites me to attend his feast and I am the last one to come, I would feel shameful. We are invited by the Lord to His table, so we have to come on time. If we all come on time, the meeting will be very much strengthened.

BEING SEATED PROPERLY IN THE MEETING

Sometimes, the way we seat ourselves in the Lord's table meeting is too poor. At times there are many people on one side of the room and empty seats on the other, without any balance. It is hard for those who sit in the corner to hear the meeting. We all should learn how to seat ourselves when we come to the meeting. If we are the first ones to come to the meeting, we should sit in the front, a section at a time. Those that come next should fill in the second rows, and those who come afterward can fill the remaining rows. To fill the seats in a proper order truly strengthens the meeting. When we arrive in the meeting, we should look at the situation and know where to sit. This is why we ask some brothers to be ushers.

We all love the church, and we love the Lord. In order to have a proper church life, we must learn to care for these practical matters, even though they are small.

PRAYING AND ANNOUNCING HYMNS IN A PROPER WAY

Third, we must learn to speak audibly in the meeting. When we pray, we have to exercise both our spirit and our voice so that others may hear. We need to take care of others' ears. To announce a hymn weakly, for example, damages, kills, and quenches the meeting. When we announce a hymn, we have to announce it loudly and properly.

We should learn the above small matters so that the Lord's table meeting will not have weaknesses. All the attendants should come on time; it is good even to come five minutes before the scheduled time. Then we should learn to seat ourselves in a proper way and pray and speak in a way that everyone can hear. These matters will help the meeting very much.

PROPERLY BEARING THE RESPONSIBILITY IN THE MEETING

Even if the brothers and sisters come to the Lord's table meeting on time and seat themselves properly, they may still not be ready in their spirit. If there is not much exercise of the spirit, if the spirit of all the attendants is dormant, we can all sense it.

The shortcomings in the table meeting are due to the

silence of those who should be bearing the responsibility. At times, the sisters function too much because the brothers are late or "buried" when they come. If the brothers are "buried," it is hard for them to care for the weaker ones. In this case, the weaker ones come in to take their place. This is the fault not of those who function incorrectly but of those who do nothing, who do not bear the responsibility for the meeting. If those brothers who should bear the responsibility do not do their duty, that becomes the weak point of the meeting. They should not complain about those who function wrongly. The two feet have to function, but if the feet do not function, the two ears will take the responsibility to walk. This creates a problem.

The biggest mistake in the Lord's table meeting may be that many who should share the responsibility do not do their job; they just "retire." Because too many retire, the wrong functioning comes out. If certain ones retire from their responsibility, we must then exercise our spirit to rescue the meeting, to bring the meeting back from being lost. We all need to learn, to be trained, and to practice these things.

HAVING A GOOD START TO THE MEETING

Basketball players realize that in order to play a good game, they must have a good start. If they start the game in the wrong way, they will lose. We all have to learn how to start the Lord's table meeting. It is not easy to call the first hymn. To begin with the hymn "Down from His Glory," for example, may start the meeting with a low atmosphere, and once the meeting is "buried" by the first hymn, it is hard to resurrect it.

At least a few minutes before the scheduled start of the meeting, the brothers should start to pray rather than announce a hymn. This will immediately bring the meeting into the right feeling. However, many keep the regulation and wait until the scheduled time to begin the meeting. Someone should offer a praise to the Lord, and then some others should follow. We need not start the meeting with a hymn, according to a regulation; rather, we should start it in a living way. That will change the whole atmosphere. It is not easy to choose a hymn to begin the meeting. Instead, we should simply learn to have some prayer.

It is easy to start a message meeting by announcing a hymn, but it is hard to start the Lord's table meeting with a hymn. It is difficult to say why this is so, but we know this from experience. Therefore, we must learn to start the table meeting by prayer, unless someone has the assurance that a certain hymn is right to start the meeting. Without the assurance, however, we should not do this. Only the proper hymn can prepare the way for a proper meeting, so unless we are very clear and the meeting is already very open and uplifted, it is better not to choose a hymn at first.

If the meeting starts in a wrong way, there is no need to adjust or correct directly. Rather, we should try the best to have another start. We may have the sense that the first hymn chosen is wrong, but we may not do anything to help the beginning of the meeting. That is simply a further mistake. After a wrong start, we have to do something right away to have the right start. This will save the meeting. If we let it go, the meeting will "float" without the proper direction.

Sometimes also we do not sense the right time to pass the bread and the cup. To pass the bread and the cup requires the right atmosphere. Otherwise, it is merely a kind of procedure or regulation. A meeting for the Lord's table that is out of the proper order is very poor. In such a case, some may still have the boldness to express something, but they may not have the flow or direction.

USING HYMNS THAT HAVE THE PROPER FEELING

During the worship of the Father, we should not sing hymns that have differing feelings. Certain hymns may even be similar, but this does not mean they match each other. One hymn may be on the greatness of God, while another is on the newness of the Father. One may be compared to the winter, another may be like the summer, and others like the spring and the fall. To sing of all "four seasons" is not to have the proper direction. We should know where the flow is going and what direction of the compass to "sail our boat."

First Corinthians 11:26 says, "For as often as you eat this

bread and drink the cup, you declare the Lord's death until He comes." In this short verse there are three points: to eat and to drink; to declare, display, and proclaim the death of Christ; and to look forward to His coming back. At the Lord's table, therefore, we always eat and drink the Lord to enjoy Him, and we display the death of Christ. Moreover, we have the sense in the spirit that as the table meeting ends, we are looking forward to His coming back. If we do have this sense, then it helps to sing some hymns about the Lord's second coming, the hope of glory. However, it is possible to call a hymn on the Lord's coming without the proper sense. This is why we stress that we need to follow the flow. To call a hymn on the Lord's coming without the flow is merely a legality; it is like serving a cold dish of food.

CARING FIRST FOR THE INNER SENSE, AND THEN FOR OUR KNOWLEDGE

Certain hymns are good to use near the beginning of the meeting because they contain no particular subject. After singing such a hymn, the right thing to do is to have some prayers in order to seek for the Lord's guidance. We may not be assured about the direction of the meeting, so we simply come to the Lord to seek and feel for the direction. In a certain prayer, we may all sense the flow and know that this is the point we should hit in that meeting. At this point, to call the wrong hymn will bring down and disturb the meeting, and the saints will not know which direction to go. We need to learn these principles.

Certain ones may call a hymn that is not fitting because they neglect the sense, the feeling, within. We all must learn that in our spiritual coordination, knowledge is not the first thing we need. The first thing we need is our sense and feeling. We have to follow the flow, the atmosphere, of the meeting by our sense, not by our knowledge. Then after we sense something, we can exercise our knowledge to either express a prayer or choose a hymn to fit what we sense.

Sometimes the sense of the spirit in the meeting is very general, and there may be no definite sense from the very beginning of the meeting to the end. At that time, we should not categorize the exact feeling in the meeting. We should simply use the hymns and even pray in a general way. That will express what is in the spirit of all the saints. When we express a general feeling, all the spirits of the saints will say amen. We may, for example, sing hymns concerning the sweetness of the Lord in a general way. There is no need to say that the Lord is the reality of the offerings or that He is food to us. We can simply enjoy the sweetness and freshness of the Lord in a general way. To emphasize that the Lord is the offerings may be too strong and definite at that time. At such a time, to sing a hymn with a definite subject is too much, and to repeat it is worse. To call such a hymn is due to functioning according to knowledge without the exercise of the inner sense.

I say again that in order to follow the flow in the meeting, the first matter is not to exercise our knowledge but to exercise the spirit. We may use the temperature of the air to illustrate the exercise of the sense followed by the exercise of knowledge. To feel that it is hot is not a matter of knowledge. It is simply something we feel. Even a little baby who does not know the word *hot* will react if he feels too hot. This is a matter of feeling, of sense. After we have the sense, however, we need a certain kind of knowledge to know what to do. After we sense the heat, we have to exercise our knowledge to know the exact temperature and to decide whether to wear spring, fall, or summer clothing. This is the proper use of knowledge. First we exercise our sense, and then we exercise our knowledge to do something that fits the sense. This is the right way to follow the flow in the meeting.

BEING LED BY THE SPIRIT TO DIFFERENT LINES IN THE MEETING

Some may move according to the teaching that we have to keep the same subject in the meeting, without checking with the inner sense. Sometimes, however, the Holy Spirit would lead us in one line and then go on to another line. This is very meaningful. In some meetings I have been in, we were on the line of the Lord's ascension at the start of the meeting. The flow was very clear, and right away we began in a high way, in ascension; then after one or two hymns and some prayers, there was the sense that the ascended Christ as the heave offering is our enjoyment today. The way to connect these two lines is mostly by prayer. We may pray, "Lord, You are the ascended One enthroned with all authority in the heavens and on the earth. Yet, Lord, You are within us to be enjoyed by us day by day as our food." Spontaneously we apply the ascended Christ, the heave offering, as our enjoyment. If we have the proper preparation through learning, the Holy Spirit will move among us in a free way.

I have been in this kind of meeting. As we enjoyed the Lord very much, a sister prayed, "O Lord, the more we enjoy You, the more we are transformed into Your image," or "The more we enjoy You, the more we are one with You in the heavens." This kind of prayer brought us into the heavens. Then right away one or two hymns followed this prayer. While we are in the heavens with the Lord, a prayer may follow to say, "O Lord, we are not only on this earth enjoying You as our food and drink, but we are one with You in the heavens." At such a time, to stay on one subject is like playing one note on an instrument; that is not music. To play different notes on different levels is music.

The practice requires learning and preparation on our part. On the one hand, we can critique our meetings, but on the other hand, I am happy because I see improvement. However, we still have to learn more. The Holy Spirit needs our coordination. If we have the proper preparation, then in the meeting when we see the Lord as the heave offering lifted up to the heavens, spontaneously within us there may be the feeling: "O Lord, You are so high, yet today You are also small, near, and available within us." In this way we bring the Lord down into our enjoyment. After praying in this way, we can exercise our spirit to choose a hymn about the Lord as food and drink.

Sometimes we may start from the point that the Lord is ascended, glorified, and enthroned, but the Holy Spirit may guide and lead us to review the Lord's life. We may spontaneously have the deep feeling to say, "Lord, Your glory today reflects Your sufferings in the past." In this way we come to the cross to see the sufferings of the Lord on the earth. This is very meaningful. We should not think that we always need to be on the line of ascension.

We need to keep these points in mind and put them into practice, especially in the Lord's table meeting. We must first exercise the inner sense to sense the atmosphere, and then we should exercise our knowledge to do something, to express something, such as choosing a hymn to fit what we sense. One brother may express something, and many others will express the same thing. This is because they are in the flow, having the same feeling.

NOT BEING DORMANT IN THE MEETING BUT BEING PREPARED TO FUNCTION

At the time for passing the bread and the cup, the brothers may be "sleeping" and not ready to function. The right hymn may be lacking, and there may not be the adequate prayers to bring the meeting into the sense that it is time for the bread and the cup to be passed. This forces the same one who started the meeting to function again. That person may be clear about which hymn to call, but he may not be the right person to do it. The right person must do it. It is even wonderful if a younger person would call the hymn. Again, we lack the proper sense and learning. If the members of a basketball team had the adequate learning, they would know how to play the game, and at a certain point they would know the right thing to do.

OUR PROPER PRAYERS REQUIRING THE PROPER CONCEPT AND UNDERSTANDING

After someone calls a hymn on life, there may not be the adequate prayers to follow it. When we sing about the love of God or the greatness of God, we have much to say, although this concept of love may not be spiritual but natural. When we sing about life, however, our mouths may be shut. This is our shortage. *Hymns,* #12 begins, "O God, Thou art the source of life, / Divine, and rich, and free! / As living water flowing out / Unto eternity!" This is altogether against our natural concept. Twenty-five or thirty years ago this was a foreign language to me. I did not know what this meant. If we have no concept of what that hymn means, we will not be able to offer a prayer to follow it. Stanza 2 says, "In love Thou in the Son didst flow / Among the human race." We may know a little bit about love, but we may not know what is meant by *Thou in the Son didst flow*. In this case, we will not be able to follow the hymn with prayer, because we do not have this kind of concept and understanding. From now on, however, we will learn more and more. Then when we announce and sing this kind of hymn, right away we will have many prayers to follow it and to analyze, enlarge, and develop its meaning.

DISTINGUISHING THE TITLES OF THE FATHER AND OF THE LORD

While we are in the section of the remembrance of the Lord, for someone to direct a prayer to the Father is a disturbance to the flow. Such a use of the title *Father* is due to our habit of praying in the past. In the same way, in the section of worship to the Father, some use the title *Lord* in their prayer. To address the Father as the Lord is not a serious mistake, but if possible, it is better to say, "Father." Generally speaking, when we mention the Lord, we mainly mean the Lord Jesus. Due to our habit in our prayer, it is easy to say "Lord"; it is not our custom to say, "Abba Father." We have to learn more, and we have to practice more. Then we will have better meetings, and we will give more cooperation to the Holy Spirit.

THE PRACTICE OF THE MEETINGS BEING VITAL FOR THE CHURCH LIFE

How to practice and conduct ourselves in the meetings is a very important matter in the church life. Christians depend very much on the meetings to be edified, perfected, and built up. If we have a living meeting, a meeting that is rich, strengthening, reigning, and in the spirit, then when people come to the meeting, they will be enriched not merely by the message but by the meeting itself. It is in the meeting that there is something living, real, and strong. Therefore, because the church life relies very much on the church meetings, we have to pay our full attention to the meetings in order to practice the church life. A meeting that is poor, low, and weak damages the church life.

In the past two and a half years here in Los Angeles we have come to realize how much the meetings mean to the church life, and how much they help people and bring people into the church life. A meeting that is proper, living, reigning, and strengthening attracts people. Once they get into the meeting, they are caught. However, a meeting that is low, weak, dull, and poor will cause people to be despondent after the first time they come. Because the meeting has nothing for them, they will not see any reason to come again.

We may be very spiritual persons, but we still may not know how to handle the meeting. We may not know how to exercise the spirit and behave in the spirit in the meeting. If this is the case, then even if we are spiritual, the poor meeting will damage the church life. We must have the Lord's table meeting in a proper, living, strengthening, edifying, and attractive way. Once people come into such a meeting, they will be attracted, caught, and edified. Therefore, we all have to learn this one thing. In order to practice the church life, we must learn how to meet together; otherwise, the church can never be built up. We all have to endeavor by the grace of the Lord to bear the responsibility for the meeting by exercising our spirit.

ABOUT THE AUTHOR

Witness Lee was born in 1905 in northern China and raised in a Christian family. At age 19 he was fully captured for Christ and immediately consecrated himself to preach the gospel for the rest of his life. Early in his service, he met Watchman Nee, a renowned preacher, teacher, and writer. Witness Lee labored together with Watchman Nee under his direction. In 1934 Watchman Nee entrusted Witness Lee with the responsibility for his publication operation, called the Shanghai Gospel Bookroom.

Prior to the Communist takeover in 1949, Witness Lee was sent by Watchman Nee and his other co-workers to Taiwan to insure that the things delivered to them by the Lord would not be lost. Watchman Nee instructed Witness Lee to continue the former's publishing operation abroad as the Taiwan Gospel Bookroom, which has been publicly recognized as the publisher of Watchman Nee's works outside China. Witness Lee's work in Taiwan manifested the Lord's abundant blessing. From a mere 350 believers, newly fled from the mainland, the churches in Taiwan grew to 20,000 in five years.

In 1962 Witness Lee felt led of the Lord to come to the United States, settling in California. During his 35 years of service in the U.S., he ministered in weekly meetings and weekend conferences, delivering several thousand spoken messages. Much of his speaking has since been published as over 400 titles. Many of these have been translated into over fourteen languages. He gave his last public conference in February 1997 at the age of 91.

He leaves behind a prolific presentation of the truth in the Bible. His major work, *Life-study of the Bible,* comprises over 25,000 pages of commentary on every book of the Bible from the perspective of the believers' enjoyment and experience of God's divine life in Christ through the Holy Spirit. Witness Lee was the chief editor of a new translation of the New Testament into Chinese called the Recovery Version and directed the translation of the same into English. The Recovery Version also appears in a number of other languages. He provided an extensive body of footnotes, outlines, and spiritual cross references. A radio broadcast of his messages can be heard on Christian radio stations in the United States. In 1965 Witness Lee founded Living Stream Ministry, a non-profit corporation, located in Anaheim, California, which officially presents his and Watchman Nee's ministry.

Witness Lee's ministry emphasizes the experience of Christ as life and the practical oneness of the believers as the Body of Christ. Stressing the importance of attending to both these matters, he led the churches under his care to grow in Christian life and function. He was unbending in his conviction that God's goal is not narrow sectarianism but the Body of Christ. In time, believers began to meet simply as the church in their localities in response to this conviction. In recent years a number of new churches have been raised up in Russia and in many eastern European countries.

OTHER BOOKS PUBLISHED BY
Living Stream Ministry

Titles by Witness Lee:

Abraham—Called by God	0-7363-0359-6
The Experience of Life	0-87083-417-7
The Knowledge of Life	0-87083-419-3
The Tree of Life	0-87083-300-6
The Economy of God	0-87083-415-0
The Divine Economy	0-87083-268-9
God's New Testament Economy	0-87083-199-2
The World Situation and God's Move	0-87083-092-9
Christ vs. Religion	0-87083-010-4
The All-inclusive Christ	0-87083-020-1
Gospel Outlines	0-87083-039-2
Character	0-87083-322-7
The Secret of Experiencing Christ	0-87083-227-1
The Life and Way for the Practice of the Church Life	0-87083-785-0
The Basic Revelation in the Holy Scriptures	0-87083-105-4
The Crucial Revelation of Life in the Scriptures	0-87083-372-3
The Spirit with Our Spirit	0-87083-798-2
Christ as the Reality	0-87083-047-3
The Central Line of the Divine Revelation	0-87083-960-8
The Full Knowledge of the Word of God	0-87083-289-1
Watchman Nee—A Seer of the Divine Revelation ...	0-87083-625-0

Titles by Watchman Nee:

How to Study the Bible	0-7363-0407-X
God's Overcomers	0-7363-0433-9
The New Covenant	0-7363-0088-0
The Spiritual Man 3 volumes	0-7363-0269-7
Authority and Submission	0-7363-0185-2
The Overcoming Life	1-57593-817-0
The Glorious Church	0-87083-745-1
The Prayer Ministry of the Church	0-87083-860-1
The Breaking of the Outer Man and the Release ...	1-57593-955-X
The Mystery of Christ	1-57593-954-1
The God of Abraham, Isaac, and Jacob	0-87083-932-2
The Song of Songs	0-87083-872-5
The Gospel of God 2 volumes	1-57593-953-3
The Normal Christian Church Life	0-87083-027-9
The Character of the Lord's Worker	1-57593-322-5
The Normal Christian Faith	0-87083-748-6
Watchman Nee's Testimony	0-87083-051-1

Available at
Christian bookstores, or contact Living Stream Ministry
2431 W. La Palma Ave. • Anaheim, CA 92801
1-800-549-5164   •   www.livingstream.com